APOCALYPSO

APOCALYPSO

Evelyn Reilly

Roof Books
New York

ISBN: 978-1-931824-45-3
Library of Congress Catalog Card Number: 2012931679

Cover design by Matthew McNerney/Polemic Design
Cover painting: *Fall of the Rebel Angels* by Pieter Bruegel the Elder
Author photograph by Greg Fuchs

to the Occupiers

Acknowledgements
An earlier version of "Dreamquest Malware," section one, appeared in Jacket2. "Childe Rolanda, or The Whatever Epic" was published by Verse.

This book was made possible, in part, with public funds from the New York State Council on the Arts, a state agency.

Roof Books are distributed by
Small Press Distribution
1341 Seventh Street
Berkeley, CA. 94710-1403
Phone orders: 800-869-7553
www.spdbooks.org

Roof Books are published by
Segue Foundation
300 Bowery
New York, NY 10012
seguefoundation.com

DREAMQUEST MALWARE

Throughout history, advances in materials
have been the basis for advances in civilization.
Metallurgy brought us from the Stone Age
to the Bronze Age. Semiconductors and magnetic materials
led us from the Industrial Age to the Information Age.
Materials that we cannot now imagine
will form the basis of devices and applications
in a future about which we can now only dream.

The Materials Sciences Division

ONE

Time stamp: ZMT 77104
Report from build site: 423

It is windy terrible and the time frame comfort slot
so doted over
keeps hurtling

today: 12 chapped columns
3 quartered globes
244 knuckled sheets

and the scalped dome project “lays wavers”

Astonishingly the corner tear is back-lit in dreamlight
and this night after night

Still we keep pouring digital spit into this blog storage device

having unboxed the urbox *permanently*

yours, sincerely

Time stamp: ZMT 77243
Report from build site: 8255

Ms. T,

It was a shock that you would send
this ignition system

instead of the slogan-infestation compress
we had so explicitly requested

What exactly was your intent?

Nonetheless we animated the chamber
and discovered the delicate filigree
of the disaster end

—a very affordable solution!

Now we can display the entire series:

barbarism star, barbarism square, barbarism float debris

Time stamp: ZMT 80002
Report from build site: 3 (one of the originals)

The signal is so sticky with procedure dreck
we grow desperate
for dislocation lubricant

Yet today we completed
2 fulfillment interstices
and 6 perfusion upsinks

after which it took hours to adjust
the nose cone of rampant grief

We have now pried countless tender chordate features
from the slab encasement

105 translation blockages
79 embedded snares

kneeling

yrs

Time stamp: ZMT 80191
Report from build site: 932

So it was that we removed
a plethora (how I love the word)
of veiled impediment confluences

This gave some relief gaze
to our personal crawl space

the previous flow
having been misinterpreted
as *openness*

Time stamp: ZMT 82048
Report from build site: 733 (also known as Glove Stab)

Yet more ugly workdays marked
by ceaseless moral deficiency showers
of which however
our terror has lessened

Many just let the face fall
into a skinflap of personal life

This is why I decided to erect the pity stations
so that each could enact their sorrow intact

44 liquid squares
3000 circumvention rods
2 mush buildings

Time stamp: ZMT 86113
Report from build site: 47

Today each program-type error
conveniently took place
on one of 1001 “moment balconies”

and for a minute I wanted to write
monumental ballets

(the auto-error demon
intervening here)

Restart then:

93 extrusion perfections
312 atonement antennas

I am so lonely
I’ve been talking to my software
for three years

Time stamp: ZMT 96927
Report from build site: 037

I am writing regarding our disposal procedures
especially for large containers
rigid with organic grief

Dinner and then breakfast as they trucked them through

(our ability to get over this)
(can even adjust to it)

Time stamp: ZMT 99999 (a moment of celestial concurrence)
Report from build site: 672

And then, finally, improvements!

Brighter dimmers replaced the blighted meters
and the blinded windows
were given decorative grills

Even the situation drive restarted
which had exhausted us for weeks

So today the sun is ambulatory! the planet ambulatory!

The surplus bark in spite of snow
peels in permeable tentacles of façade plu!

Time stamp: ZMT 100249
Report from build site: 3774

Well, the address tower finally overlooks
the management stations

and a panel laid against
the edge condition

marks the site for touristic pilgrimage

So many kinds of pulverized material:
I fill the vials out of some sense
of future retrieval

Just don't breathe and the dust
won't get over you

Time stamp: ZMT 107713
Report from build site: as of yet unnumbered

Thus our continuing dilemma

the whole heritage of tower
approach, assertion, lure

power and the views

And in the end this sober landscape

littered with so much
dreamware wreckage

(check the annals
re heavy wing black cast)

all that was once rated
triple E for excellent

TWO

TO: The Authorities
RE: Cumulo Cirrus

Variation in days   clear unclear clear clear abandoned

The proposed paper fairness cones
appear to be attractive and supportive

and will be used (as suggested) in the service
of our collective ecstatic devotion practice

TO: The Authorities
RE: Civil Seriousness

So we are now a people and call ourselves “the people”
going home on a compressed path
toward the vision replacement apparition

(but whether it is destroyed or just shrinks
upon approach still confuses)

TO: The Authorities
RE: Dismissals

Telling them again and again: STAY

intruding into limp corridors to find the stump ends

for we are social and the animals are

blown fragments

TO: The Authorities
RE: Misdemeanors

In spite of the coup data
the assets estimate
allows a certain slipframe

into which I inserted this thin reform gadget

total brittlement

then to my surprise
a milder fragrance of *duration*

TO: The Authorities
RE: Public Inquisition

They wanted us to be witnesses, spread out the materials

Drawers and drawers of dreamware evidence

TO: The Unanswerers
RE: Concurring Ashes

Another memorial today:

(bottomless tower bottomless drawer)

and the species so hyper-emotional

Still, the slab advisor says "optimistic"

TO: The Unauthorized
RE: Final Submission

An aching distance
still forms the basis

of our ravish
hybrid
repertory

(a quest
that became an anti-
epic)

But what lay in the midst
except the tower itself?

and fields

of unintended
result flowers

CHILLED HAROLD

Having drawn
something to walk on,

a straight path
to avoid getting lost,

Harold lost his way.
He took a short cut

to where a forest
was supposed to be,

and found one remaining tree,
with fruit needing protection.

So he drew some fierce protection
and got so caught up

in the violence of his depiction,
he scared even himself.

Shaking, he drew the ripples
of a sea by accident,

then quickly got in over his head.
Eventually, he climbed onto some sand,

where a sign said "Reserved for American
Picnic" before an astonishing spread.

He ate a huge amount of appalling pie,
and then shared the rest with a moose

and a deserving porcupine,
leaving the undeserving porcupines

cold and hungry, because now Harold
was drawing a mountain

from which to locate the window
of a room he misremembered

as a place of perfect refuge.
This image so distracted him,

he walked straight off a cliff.
Frantically he drew rescue vehicles,

none of which stopped his rapid descent,
until he engineered a balloon

that brought him down before a home
he didn't know he'd been looking for,

although his companion, Chatty Cathy,
had been talking about it

for some time now. The balloon sat
in the wet grass of a house that

was nothing like what they had in mind,
but was where they had landed.

Behind it tall buildings were rising
in a city of fire escapes

with glamorous figures ascending
and descending. One stood on a high step

speaking a strange utopian language,
and Harold grew nervous

about her foothold on such a thin ledge.
He was about to call out,

when a passing policeman
told him to just continue

in the direction he was heading.
There is no refuge, Silly Putty,

said his new friends, who had come
down from the fire escapes

to reveal themselves as strangers
enamored with the word community.

You must mean social networking,
said one with a tight smile

standing off to the side.
This was a development Harold

had missed while obsessed
with a path that was growing

more and more like an inscrutable
branching diagram. He was, of course,

lost all over again as the ambiguous
thicket muffled the words

of the utopian strangers and concealed
the widespread porcupine hunger.

Soon the towers of the developers
overshadowed the low windows

of rooms that had once been filled
with silver pools of purple moon.

Dauntless, Child Harold picked up
his darkest crayon and drew.

NATURE FUTURISM

POWDERY FLOWERS

1.

Unravel the corner
through a bloom section
and the I-thought spills into continuous plural flow

a conversation coated

with flower scum lip profusion flavor

2.

Transient pigment
fingering light petals

and shoes

one shoe   pathos

one

the suffering of the innocents

and the third

striding the parapets

to examine the newly-installed
junk tower caryatids

3.

This is the correspondence, then, of visual dialog

in the space we have been having

4.

What could we have been thinking?

(optimism ammunition cases
filled in the middle of the night)

No we are still all right and will be maybe

(scrawls remain)

5.

So many bodies setting off detectors

this is the meek and the lame

6.

Well, things change and change quickly races
along the perpetual movement track

propelling discontinuous leapings
in the singed
but not entirely extirpated
grass-like substance

7.

Why what repeats itself repeats
Why what repeats repeats the self-replicatory system

plus random mutation messaging:

TAA ATC CAG
ATT TAG GTC

and the oracle says “offending command: syntax error”

8.

So we went ahead and inserted the sequence
being in dire need of bugs and fleurs

CLIMATE MEMORY

1.

In the pockets between void material

v is for victory (vacated)
v for validation (evacuated)

vv for our very pretty
but metallic-tasting

rain

in which I found a tiny nozzle with a love set inflow valve

and a "write-to-lift" feature intact

2.

So I quietly heaved myself up
into a special calling

in the background of which some scaffolded script:

plantgoo (this is a true actual transcription—

But what does this casual flower
inaugurate?

3.

Shock one was the ignition torch (I mean touch)
two the blithe extermination fee
(I mean feel)

We are awash
in premonition

4.

Sure there remains a floortrap for the sorrow
which you can choose to keep clean or not

Leaves an aftersmear

(is really pretty shocking)

5.

But do not underestimate the power
of how what grew there did

The throat opens and captures
the thrown down
error signal repeat phrases

6.

Against this faux environment
total and extreme

shadows of a procession
across an archaic memory screen

cow, drone, excess

Then we constructed
a touchable
beflowered surface

and confirmed our status
as a site of virtual
natural
heritage

ROBIN CITRUS

1.

Robin emerges from a file called "wet"

memory of *wet*
something called *true wet*

now the entire file is called "coaxial wet robin"

(two conductors
separated by a common insulator)

2.

cannot expose cannot
material for material
in darkness into the corners

cannot expose cannot
the material in darkets
for the four corners

blow down small rain (coldest poem)

Ok, but where to shred the ribbon?

3.

“The rending of the clothes expresses the deepest feelings
of sorrow and anguish.

How shallow, how disappointing, how pitiably trivial, therefore,
to symbolize these authentic sentiments by a little button.”

4.

broken ear cornucopia outlet
and dim utility escape hatch

Was sad *poetically*

(rent ribbon

5.

among button translation fevers

translation lever clasp commas

6.

communication schemes
over the lip of which

we *touched on* today

7.

Howls through the night here

Wormy gardenia with flies, Miss July

8.

campanula primrose quarantine stickers
hanging on threads in all the vehicles

9.

It was the grief then must interrupt
and permeate the *true writing*

So you know the place   species memory?   robin anachronism family?

Where did that emerge from?

memory, nostalgic/analgesic

Robin citrus, the lexicon of one post-industrial life form chariot

10.

The mourner should make a tear in the proper clothing upon her return home.

CHILDE ROLANDA, or THE WHATEVER EPIC

Here endeth, then,
Progress this way

Robert Browning,
Childe Harold to the Dark Tower Came

Names in my ears

all the lost

the Spring My Heart Made

sudden river trickle

and charged rain

epistolary pistils

along a Path Darkening

Rain ampules

liquid word phials

came to arrest my thoughts

Questions that CrackDevastate

the extreme corner of the page

no scale order or end

to this series

Wheel which gets the wormiest

sticker panels Nightingale

Panels Small Still Voice

and total inversion splash ruin

in the strictest sense

of the personal desire party

but saddle ached

saddle ached and ached

This was the place Crayola

the Loretto Laredo

where even those

Who Could Find in Their List

trembling outcomes

old man of which

engine trouble

and the interface touch

a little bit dated

Although the View the Same

migrating into the deepest pocket

of Next Phase Phrases

a switch of the Thin New

once upper

now “in it” low

and Subject to the Same Error

In Middle Ground

Tall Scalped Mountain

and lame figure in the cleft

sunset where Noise was Named Ears

re-spoken in the muffle

of horror ardor and blond worry

The Arm That Will Reach Out

when dry blades prick the mud

For flowers fill cruel rents

with Environmental Trial Run

natural regrowth material

mostly alien mostly waste

but coherent with alarms

that Bruise the Creature Program

alert the disappearing progress memo

laid down millennia and millennia

And She Whose She-Horn is also

a camera also a navigational device

photographs as a Breathing Rock

what was picked up as a speaking sea

of avant jewelry: rock paper scissor

and Uber Fern Leaking Through

so many pre-set talking points

disambiguated among the creeping forces

of multiple password panic

in which dauntless Childe Rolanda

whistle blower forest format maven

trolling the underside

of the Universal Mistake Blanket

presses to lipless lips

the endzone slugfest

run out of fuel last lines

(locust marrow sepal

sorrow) of the Whatever Epic

APOCALYPSO: A COMEDY

a•poc•a•lypse

the complete and final destruction of the world,
especially as described in the biblical book of Revelation

(Gk., *apokálypsis*, "lifting of the veil")

Whosoever is not found written in the book of life
will be cast into the lake of fire.

Revelations 20.15

Thus strange verb tenses must be enacted:
these are those things that *will have had to have been,*
that *will have had to yet occur.*

BARGE (Bay Area Research Group in Enviro-aesthetics)

And I became the Alpha
and the Omega

and my little dog too

Come and I'll show you what once
shall have taken place after this

forever and ever and ever, etc.

at which I took my glue gun
from its hipster holster

and twenty-four elders
began to sing:

Eight swimming creatures covered with eyes (state of the oceans, check)
Sixteen birds with sinister wings (state of the flyways, checkers)

But even the end of evolve, luv?   (I was down with the animals)

Then the twenty-four fell down:
clad in white garments
and wearing golden crowns

(this is the revised standard
sedition edition chapter four
verses one through ten

in which enumeration equals

a technique of *calm*

3 2 1   we are calm

So many pretty revels
in these devastation pictures

head as mollusk shell
whale with insect tail

and a twig become
a tiny musician
fingering a stringy box

(see *Fall of the Rebel Angels*
by Pieter Bruegel)

as I scan
my es-cat-a-logue

covering that part of the language
concerned with reckoning
and the density destiny
of survivor species

For he poured his bowls of wrath on the earth
and a great star fell onto the rivers

This sympathy
is a revelation too

I greet you as friends, every one
I know your faith
and patient endurance

But this is my complaint
and counter-argument:

That he has abandoned the love
he had at first

and unleashed the dog
of my darkest humor
to devour the chapters
that verseth

(with apologies to *Canis familiarus*—
a family of deep-chested mammals
with long strides who hunt
by pursuing prey
over great distances
until it eventually tires)

Come over lover rover
help spread some phoenix ashes
in this bit of ravaged woods

I will war against you with my sword mouth, he says
a threat I ignore
in chapter two verse twelve

that orifice having been removed from the list
of body parts requiring medical attention

(to eat, speak, suck, lick
thus not covered
by real insurance)

The gape of agape
disarmed these days

I will spew you out
(this is chapter three verse sixteen)
because you are lukewarm

because you are a lukewarm worm
of the Phylum Annelid
among the grass and the lilies
(Order Liliales, Genus Lilium)

And how by being anxious
can a warm worm add one cubit
to this span of life?

(This is his "good cop" voice)

Do not be tense for tomorrow,
he says, *nothing dates faster*
than the present future

So I turn instead to the rap *of him*
who has the seven spirits
and the seven rats

oops, cancel that translit-
eration, of course it's *stars* (r-a-t-s plus one extra s)

For vermin *you are the name of being alive*
(this is chapter three verse one)

and I mean to vindicate the innocent
and address vermin love words

to the seven rats of the seven stars

(3 2 1   I am calm

before this bill of $450 for setting the traps
plus one return visit for final inspection

"I can smell them when they are present,"
the very nice exterminator said.)

Here's a favorite poem
rediscovered at ubuweb.com

Garbage Event, Daybreak, Borneo

1. Pigs and chickens feed on the grass
in an inhabited area until it is bare of grass.
2. Garbage is added to the area.
3. The participants defend the "abandoned beauty"
and "town-quality" of the environment against all critics.

For we have stepped into the sacred areas
and wept over our waste procedures

which is will have been being our transcendence

(This is the revels
shared *common*-ly)

Now back to our story of tribulation endurance
or is it tribal divergence
on this island *most pat* —

as we are just about to cross
the George Washington Bridge:

Excuse me,
a question while we are driving
I sd., John, I sd
what do you have anyway
against historical time?

Disturbed just a bit today
by my own privilege screen
comfort mechanisms —
swear to smash their cockroach footprints

But delete this derogation
of Phylum Arthropod
Order Blattaria

with so many genera
including the oriental roach
(*Blatta orientalis*) and the American
(*Periplaneta americana*)

and some, especially in the genus Ectobius,

which are "small temperate species that live outdoors"

And in that phrase I find my home page

singing loving my vermin
singing sunniest day

dancing my aptest app-dance
under these apo-calypso rays

This morning kicking against the pricks
of wholesale legislative
abandonment

and in the distance the sirens
add some lurid backup
to these cataclysmic lyrics:

And a third of the sea became blood
a third of the living creatures died

And many were cast alive into a lake of fire
and all the fowls were filled with their flesh

(Note the touch of vulture:
which, along with the condor,
is of the family Cathartidae,
meaning *purifier*)

This evening I am feeling approximately 60% female 40% male
33% *Homo sapiens*, 33% *Serpentes squamata*
rather protista, part erectus, somewhat prostratus
or maybe mostly *Mus musculus*
genus mouse species house (our friends) —

little acrobats participating in our project
of universal plant and animal redemption

The friends greet you. Greet the friends, every one of them.

To she/he who conquers I will grant to eat of the tree of life
        (good angel) (eats the book)
To she/he who conquers the tree I will grant to eat the world
        (bad angel) (utter demolishment)
To she/he who conquers the world what a waste of time
        (eats some history is gone quickly)

We are just now passing through security
carrying as much fruit of the tree
of knowledge as possible

(how I love my Apple)

He who conquers shall not be hurt by the second death
my Crown of Life screen saver crows

and seven kings on seven thrones
are all holding lampstands
which were once the figures
of the lit circles of the beloved

(still available in many styles
and colors: Lucretian Swoon
Enlightenment Sunset
Post-Utopian Dragon's Breath)

and just now the automatic writing
starts screaming:

A third of the sun was struck
And a third of the moon
And a third of the stars
And a third of the day was kept from shining
And likewise a third of the night

This would will have been
the dimming of the bulbs

For I have this against you brand name
For I have this against you product description
For I have this against you obsession
with the whore of Babylon
in every other movie made by man

Her I hereby redesignate a victim of privilege screen
comfort mechanisms

Thus she shall be clad in white garments
and I will unblot her name in the book of life

(this is chapter three
verse five revisited)

Every morning reveals another crevice
of this denatured nature canvas

Today a sea of glass
(chapter fifteen verse two)

for they have opened the new aquarium
and embraced the principles
of my sting-ray version
of the beatitudes:

Blessed are the bottom-dwellers
who are pure among the lightless
Blessed are the predators
for they are innocent but violent

Bless the short-tailed Urolophidae
and the long-tailed Dasyatidae
including the common species
which careens around the metal tank
via undulations of its bat-like fins

And in the next the sea slugs
unearthly in fluorescent ruffles
scour the shallow waters

while above their heads *Medusa*
lowers a tangle of stinging tentacles

Nembrotha, Godiva,
Chromodoris Daphne

Let's read out of our bestiaries, beloveds

All this animal stuff is a distraction
my comrade sniffs
padding among the susurrations
of the filtration systems —

he who came in out of the cold
fifteen thousand years ago

Today it's a field day out from the usual enclosures
(Word, Facebook, Linked-in, Google)

for another all-time favorite poem:

1. A man & woman looking for lilies.
2. All the people going down to look for lilies.
3. Mud taken up looking for lilies.
4. Washing the lilies in the water to remove the mud.
5. Washing themselves off after the mud has got on them.
6. Lilies in a basket.
7. Walking from the lily place "to go look for a dry place to sit down."

Just supporting the fair use policy
of our common commons
to bless the bulbs
that feed the prairie rodents

Chapter six is extremely important
the four horses and the lamb
standing *although it had been slain*

as one person/messiah/cipher
takes the scroll from the director's hand
and elders chant a demand for ransom

to the rhythm of a ticking bomb —

and the sun becomes as sackcloth
the full moon like blood

It's all death on my wall and the more colorful for it
A big artistic impetus this endtime vision

This is excess
This is the uncalled for

while my partner keeps circling
his own tense issues

his pelt itches
he has dermatological troubles
probably resulting from long-term exposure
to environmental chemicals

6 the world's water is locked up as ice

5 massive floods of volcanic lava

4 a great rock falls from the sky

3 clouds of dust cover the sun

2 tall plants starve and animals wither

1

But we are getting rather out of order
still holding the bomb in our clock hands
I mean the tsunami I mean the flood
I mean the hurricane that pummels
the poor and the weak as a voice
in the midst of chapter six verse
eight is speaking building codes
deficient regulatory powers international
aid diversions and the darkest rider
(in both legal and equestrian senses)
flails its financial instrument vehicle
with fiscal irresponsibility reins

And a third of the waters
became wormwood
and many died
because they were made bitter

Forgive us sweet hermaphrodite
working the tainted soil

Blessed are those who toil

And the sky vanished like a scroll that is rolled up
the mountains were removed from their places
and the frail and dispossessed were left
beside girls with menstrual cramps
babies born one hour previously
and those already suffering
from skin rashes joint ailments
those who lost their medications
who never had medications
the epileptics paralytics and demoniacs
of Matthew four verse twenty-four
and sages with broken feet and eye trouble
who set up little altars in shattered corners

— a shell a twig a leaf

Now the scabbed flowers dropped
to the ground and the grass
broke into thousands of pieces

The sun was black with eagle weeping
the sea thick with apo-oceanic scum

While the privilege screen mechanisms
continued on their language mission

disclosing to certain entitled persons
things withheld from the majority
of humankind (Wikipedia
apocalypse definition two)

and allowing those with the seal
upon their foreheads
to torture the rest
for a numerologically important
number of months and years

Today the insects are arrayed as if on horses
and torture us with the noise
of their living wing chariots

One flecked with sulfur
places a delicate appendage
onto the page for half a second

Blessed are those who stridulate

And the flowers
of the apocalypse —

stalky ashen broken caked
with coral reef skeletal remnants
and the dust of lichen
that grows in the tundra

lay at the feet
of Our Lady of Apocalypso

who says no return
to that home page
while playing a steely drum

So I told him to give me the little scroll;
and he said to me, *Take, eat;*
it will be sour to your stomach,
but sweet as honey in your mouth.

And I ate the words literally
as the sirens geared up
(Class Mammalia, Order Sirenia,
with only four remaining species)

and my companion animal,
confused by the prospectus
of Cerberus Capital Management
(one of the most experienced
distressed market investors),
started barking in a frenzy
as if the world were coming to an end

At which eight armies arrayed in fine linen
(note preoccupation with luxury goods)
appeared behind an angel on a white horse
(note symbolic color markers)
and each on his collar had a name inscribed
(logos thy name is trademark)

and a call went out to the scavengers
to gather for a great supper

at which was served the flesh
of those on the side of the beast
and of the false prophet
who had worked the false signs

And beneath the howling and shrieking
a low familiar voice was singing:

The whirlwind is in the thorn tree

(I really love those late Johnny Cash CDs.)

Then he showed me the river
of the waste water of life

with trees on either side filled
with strangely identical fruit
and leaves for the healing of nations
strewn across ruined grounds

And we visited an ancient city
with gates forty-feet tall
of red and yellow stone
and remains of ramparts

more than two miles long
(much measuring
much urban planning
in chapter twenty-one)

Together we saw these things
having pooled our points
and taken advantage
of our award cards

place: city on a hill
obsession: lampstands
temporary housing: bushels

And I shivered as he said,
Everyone who is angry
with his brother shall be liable

So I called to clear up
that misunderstanding

(lucre lucre lucre)

and was put on hold

So I went on Safari to consult
the mindspring oracle

and was stymied
by a "bad gateway"

But this is a love poem anyway. It is extraordinarily physical.
I am loving my enemies. I am loving my neighbors.
I take them into my mouth. I eat their book.

(sucre sucre sucre)

And the final finch alights
on the fixation dirt
pouring its lithe breath
over the grass tips
(version one)

And the strange bird
of the emergent species
waits on the periphery
for the next decentering
(version two)

as we dip our fingers
into a language stream, cool
as an evolutionary explanation
of altruism

O sirens
O cow pasture
O rescue vehicles

ceaselessly seeking the real emergency
beneath the emergencies

This is how
what would will have been
being a diversion

merged instead
into a vision
of preliminary descent

while sleeping on your carbon cushion
Flight 267
New York from Kiev

dreaming dark diagnosis of sparrow
dreaming dim prognostication of entrails

dreaming strange guy
in the aisle seat
seemingly overwhelmed
by difficulties

(You, too, John,
should get some rest)

Thank you, friends, for your love and endurance
This is the end of our revelatory revels

NOTES

"Dreamquest Malware" integrates some faux architectural language from *Siteless: 1001 Building Forms*, by François Blanciak. The statement on page seven is taken from the website of the Materials Sciences Division of the Lawrence Berkeley National Laboratory.

Harold and the Purple Crayon, by Crockett Johnson, and "Childe Harold to the Dark Tower Came," by Robert Browning, were the inspiration for "Chilled Harold" and "Childe Rolanda," respectively. The quote on page 25 is directly from Browning.

The Chabad-Lubavitch website was the source for the statement quoted in section three of "Robin Citrus."

The call for the enactment of strange verb tenses that initiates "Apocalypso: A Comedy" is from the BARGE publication, *Buried Treasure Island: A Detour of the Future*, 2008. Angela Hume Lewandowski pointed me to Walter Benjamin's notion of the "real state of emergency," a phrase which appears in this poem. The events—"Garbage Event" and "Lily Events"—which are both incorporated into this piece, were first published in *Technicians of the Sacred*, edited by Jerome Rothenberg. They are now available at ubuweb.com.

Roof Books are published by
Segue Foundation
300 Bowery • New York, NY 10012
Visit our website at seguefoundation.com

Roof Books are distributed by
SMALL PRESS DISTRIBUTION
1341 Seventh Street • Berkeley, CA. 94710-1403.
Phone orders: 800-869-7553
spdbooks.org